For my sisters

Cover: *O Holy Night* © Simon Dewey. Courtesy of Altus Fine Art. For print information, visit www.altusfineart.com

Page iv–1: *It's a Wonderful Christmas* © Paul Landry. Courtesy of The Greenwich Workshop, Inc. www.greenwichworkshop.com

Page 2–3: *Reason for the Season* © Greg Olsen. By arrangement with Greg Olsen Art, Inc. For more information about art prints by Greg Olsen, please visit www.GregOlsen.com or call 800-352-0107

Page 4–5: *Nativity* © Annie Henrie. Courtesy of Altus Fine Art. For print information, visit www.altusfineart.com

Page 6: *Mary and Child* © Simon Dewey. Courtesy of Altus Fine Art. For print information, visit www.altusfineart.com

Pages 8–9: *Song of the Heart* © J. Kirk Richards. For print information, go to www.jkirkrichards.com

Page 10–11: *Gift* © Roger Loveless. For more information, go to www.rogerlovelessart.com

Pages 12–13: *King of Kings* © 2014 Howard Lyon. For print information, go to www.fineart.howardlyon.com or call 480.241.7907

Pages 14–15: *The Nativity* © Dona Gelsinger. For more information, visit www.gelsingerlicensing.com

Page 16–17: *A Savior Is Born* © Joseph F. Brickey. For more information, go to www.josephbrickey.com

Pages 18–19: *Love's Pure Light* © Annie Henrie. Courtesy of Altus Fine Art. For print information, visit www.altusfineart.com

Page 20–21: *O Holy Night* © Simon Dewey. Courtesy of Altus Fine Art. For print information, visit www.altusfineart.com

Pages 22–23: *A Son Is Given* © 2012 Howard Lyon. For print information, go to www.fineart.howardlyon.com or call 480.241.7907

Page 24–25: *In the Arms of Mary* © Simon Dewey. Courtesy of Altus Fine Art. For print information, visit www.altusfineart.com

Pages 26–27: *Star of Wonder* © Simon Dewey. Courtesy of Altus Fine Art. For print information, visit www.altusfineart.com

All Christmas Symbols © iStockphotography.com

Cover design copyright © 2014 by Covenant Communications, Inc.

Jacket and book designed by Christina Marcano © 2014 Covenant Communications

Published by Covenant Communications, Inc.
American Fork, Utah

Text © 2014 by Rachelle Pace Castor

Printed in China
First Printing: October 2014

21 20 19 18 17 16 15 14   10 9 8 7 6 5 4 3 2 1

ISBN: 978-1-62108-806-6

The Symbols of Christmas

Finding the Meaning in the Symbols of the Season

Rachelle Pace Castor

Sparkle, glitter, tinsel, lights—
the stores are filled with
wondrous sights.

Toys and games and sweets
piled high—
so many kinds of
gifts to buy.

Yet *hidden* in the glitz and *swirl,* beyond the loud commercial whirl are quiet *symbols* tucked away, *reminders* of that HOLY day.

when
God the Father
sent His
SON
to teach us how to
live as one.

A baby
good and
MEEK and mild—
to save
the world,
God Sent
His child.

Like the
star (that led the way)
to BABY *Jesus*
in the hay,
we can *shine*
by treating others
as our
sisters
and our brothers.

Like the
angels'
songs of GLORY
filled the skies
to tell the
story,
we sing
carols of
His birth
to share the news
with all the
earth.

Like the shepherd's
crook-neck staff
guiding lambs
along the path,
the candy cane striped
RED and WHITE
reminds His lambs
to choose the right.

Like the *gifts* the
Wise Men
brought
in *honor* of the
King they sought,
we *give* a GIFT,
and we *receive*
a deeper Love
for those in need.

Like the
wreath
hung on the door

a **symbol** of

forevermore—
even death is not
the end;
His birth *is why*
we'll *live again.*

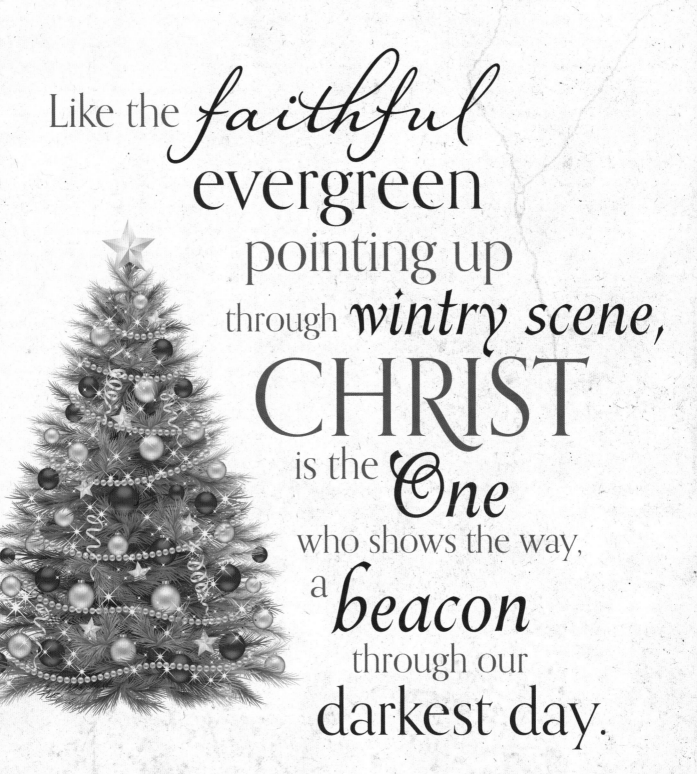

Like the *faithful* evergreen pointing up through **wintry scene,** CHRIST is the *One* who shows the way, a *beacon* through our darkest day.

Like the BELL chimes
true and clear,
CALLING us
to come and hear,
this season sends us
sweet
reminders to choose
to be a little kinder.

Like *ribbons*
wrapped and tied
with LOVE
reminding us
of HOME above,
she wrapped Him up
in swaddling
white
and held Him SAFE
throughout the night.

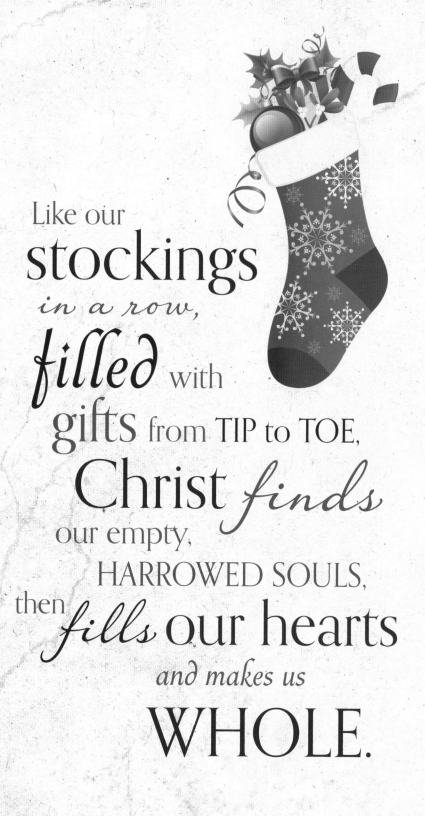

Like our
stockings
in a row,
filled with
gifts from TIP to TOE,
Christ *finds*
our empty,
HARROWED SOULS,
then *fills* our hearts
and makes us
WHOLE.

Like the *holly,*
red and green,
all creation
has foreseen
that in *His death* claim
we will have claim
on life ETERNAL
through *Christ's*
name.

This
Christmas
may we *see*
the *reason* behind
the
symbols
of the season.

Like *Jesus,*
we can do our
best to make
this day
and all the rest
like
Christmas.

Like stars and wreaths
and bells that ring,
like stockings,
trees and carols we sing,
like candy canes
and
gifts we bring,
like BOWS and
holly—red and green,
what other
symbols
can you find,
hidden at this
Christmastime?